Eastern Bluebirds

Julie Murray

Abdo Kids Junior
is an Imprint of Abdo Kids
abdobooks.com

abdobooks.com

Published by Abdo Kids, a division of ABDO, P.O. Box 398166, Minneapolis, Minnesota 55439. Copyright © 2022 by Abdo Consulting Group, Inc. International copyrights reserved in all countries. No part of this book may be reproduced in any form without written permission from the publisher. Abdo Kids Junior™ is a trademark and logo of Abdo Kids.

Printed in the United States of America, North Mankato, Minnesota.

052021

092021

Photo Credits: iStock, Minden Pictures, Shutterstock

Production Contributors: Teddy Borth, Jennie Forsberg, Grace Hansen

Design Contributors: Candice Keimig, Pakou Moua

Library of Congress Control Number: 2020947529

Publisher's Cataloging-in-Publication Data

Names: Murray, Julie, author.
Title: Eastern bluebirds / by Julie Murray
Description: Minneapolis, Minnesota : Abdo Kids, 2022 | Series: State birds | Includes online resources and index.
Identifiers: ISBN 9781098207151 (lib. bdg.) | ISBN 9781098207991 (ebook) | ISBN 9781098208417 (Read-to-Me ebook)
Subjects: LCSH: State birds--Juvenile literature. | Bluebirds--Juvenile literature. | Birds--Behavior--United States--Juvenile literature.
Classification: DDC 598.297--dc23

Eastern Bluebirds

Many eastern bluebirds live in the eastern US.

Table of Contents

Eastern Bluebirds. 4

State Bird 22

Glossary. 23

Index 24

Abdo Kids Code. 24

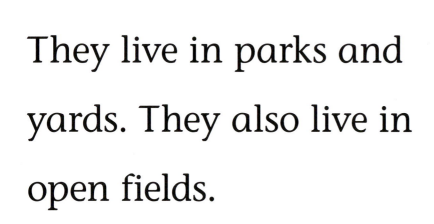

They live in parks and yards. They also live in open fields.

Males have bright blue feathers.

Females are lighter in color.

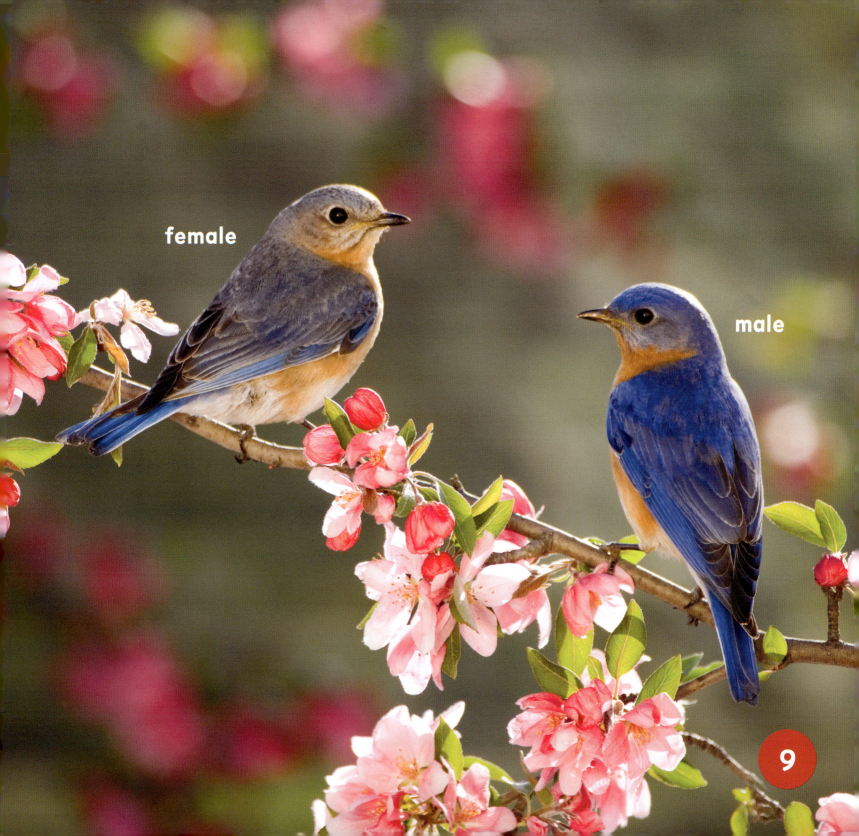

Their chests are **rust** in color. Their bellies are white.

They like to be in groups.

They sit on a **perch**.

They look for food.

They eat berries. They also
eat insects.

Their nests are in trees.

The nests are made of grass and weeds.

The bird lays 2 to 7 eggs.

Chicks hatch in 15 days.

State Bird

MO
Missouri

NY
New York

22

Glossary

chick
a bird that has just hatched or a young bird.

hatch
to come out of an egg.

perch
a branch where a bird sits.

rust
an orange or reddish-brown color.

Index

belly 10

chest 10

chicks 20

color 8

eggs 20

feathers 8

food 14, 16

habitat 6

nests 18

United States 4

Visit **abdokids.com** to access crafts, games, videos, and more!

Use Abdo Kids code **SEK7151** or scan this QR code!